COLLEGE COOKING:
Allergy-Free

COLLEGE COOKING:
ALLERGY-FREE

Jody Falco

ISBN: 978-0-9909486-0-5 (sc)
ISBN: 978-0-9909486-1-2 (e)

Because of the dynamic nature of the Internet, any web addresses or links contained in this book may have changed since publication and may no longer be valid. The views expressed in this work are solely those of the author and do not necessarily reflect the views of the publisher, and the publisher hereby disclaims any responsibility for them.

Any people depicted in stock imagery provided by Thinkstock are models, and such images are being used for illustrative purposes only. Certain stock imagery © Thinkstock.

Lulu Publishing Services rev. date: 11/23/2015

To Carlo

Wise and courageous, whose example I try to follow
And, for love and support, Jeffrey always.

CONTENTS

INTRODUCTION

I wrote this cookbook—this set of recipes—for my son as he began his first year of living off-campus. His multiple food allergies made it difficult, if not unsafe, for him to eat in the dining halls—though he did eat there for two years, mostly having lots of grilled chicken. Thank goodness for a microfridge, so he could microwave baked potatoes in his room! By year three, off-campus he went, and he bought his own groceries to cook his own meals in his own kitchen.

So, I sat down to write out these easy, safe recipes for him to make—and the result is here: **College Cooking: Allergy-Free**.

These recipes are easy-to-make meals, and all ingredients are found in any supermarket or grocery store.

Being a mom, I've also shared my opinions on essential equipment and utensils for the kitchen—as well as what items no pantry should be without: like salt and pepper! Also, being a mom, I've shared more—like notes on serving sizes, basic kitchen safety, timing and general advice that I think will help <u>any</u> cook. And, I've assumed that anyone reading this cookbook has only the barest experience in the kitchen and is, like every student, short on time.

All the recipes are made without:
Dairy * Eggs * Peanuts * Tree Nuts * Fish/
Shellfish * Wheat * Soy * Sesame

<u>No</u> recipes in this book need substitutions to be allergy-free. And all of the recipes are simple and delicious and healthy. I do note, here and there, some options for the non-food allergic: for example, use wheat pasta instead of corn, should you like.

But, first—a few words about organization.

I've arranged these recipes in alphabetical order, avoiding the traditional categories like "Soups" or "Appetizers." The names of the recipes will make it easy to see what meal it's for, and alphabetical order seemed the most sensible way for a new cook. Opposite the recipes are notes or shopping lists or suggestions about serving that dish. And, on my blog foodallergyworks.com, you'll find a section with pictures for every one of these recipes—so you can see what the dish should look like when it's ready to serve.

In the next few pages, I've suggested what are the **Essentials** in every kitchen—from spices to pots and pans. And, after the recipes, in the back, I've included a short list of terms and definitions. What does "simmer" mean anyway—and how can you tell it's simmering when you're cooking it!

I love to cook: Chopping vegetables relaxes me, experimenting with flavors intrigues me. But most of all I love to cook because feeding people gives me pleasure.

I don't think of cooking as an exact science—which is why I don't bake well—baking *is* an exact science.

Cooking is about **taste and feel** and a little bit of experiment. Do these ribs need more hot sauce? Is the steak medium rare? Let's use one tablespoon of oil instead of two. Cooking is also about personal style and taste: another shake more pepper if you like it spicy, or an extra handful of breadcrumbs in the meatloaf to stretch it, or three carrots instead of four, because you don't like orange. These small "deviations" from the recipes here will only enhance these meals and make them your own.

College Cooking: Allergy-Free gives you 25 recipes—for main courses and side dishes and SuperBowl parties. So start cooking and start eating!

I hope this cookbook shows you how to cook safe and easy meals for yourself. And, I hope it helps you to enjoy cooking.

Jody Falco
September 2015
foodallergyworks@gmail.com

And, remember, on my blog foodallergyworks.com you'll find a section with pictures for every one of these recipes—so you can see what the dish looks like when it's finished.

ESSENTIALS

Pots and Pans

I like stainless steel pots and pans: they're durable, easy to clean and conduct heat well. I do not like non-stick. Again, chef's preference here. There are "cookware starter sets"—which range wildly in price— that have a variety of pots and pans. When purchasing, get pots and pans that have a good solid feel—but are not too heavy to move around. Pots with heavier bottoms will conduct heat evenly which helps anyone to cook better.

- Frying pans: one big (9 inch) and one small(7 inch), with covers
- One-handled pot, with cover (3 quart and possibly 1 ½ quart)
- Two-handled pot, with cover (4 ½ quart and possibly 6 quart—which is really large)
- Roasting pan or baking dish—Pyrex, stainless steel, bakeware
- Casserole, round, Pyrex or bakeware
- Broiling pan—sometimes called a fajita sizzle pan, comes with a handle for broiling meats

Cookware and Utensils

- Mixing bowl(s), at least one, but can buy in "nesting" sets of three
- Measuring cup, Pyrex or plastic
- Colander or strainer
- <u>Knives:</u> The range is endless. I use: a serrated blade, like a steak knife, breadknife or ginzu. Non-serrated knives are supposed to be better for slicing meats
- Slotted Spoon and Wooden Spoon
- Spatula
- Pot holders
- Dish towels
- Cleaning supplies: steel wool pads, sponge, scrubbie, dish detergent

Spices

- Salt
- Pepper
- Olive Oil
- Vinegar (wine, apple cider, white)
- Parsley, fresh and dried
- Rosemary

<u>Other spices:</u>

Basil; Bay leaf –for stews; Cilantro; Sage—for meats

Foodstuffs

- Onions
- Garlic
- Potatoes, baking, sweet
- Carrots
- Celery
- Rice
- Pasta

<u>Canned foods</u>: Beans, Tomatoes/ tomato sauce

Carrots add sweetness; potatoes add bulk.

Stew is a very forgiving meal. It only gets better the next day as the flavors deepen.

Stew can be served hot, or warm. You can add water to make it "soupier." And you can add another can of peas and some more potatoes (cooked) to stretch it as leftovers.

Also, some people put in a Tablespoon or two of tomato sauce/paste. This flavors the stew, brings in more salt, and also helps tenderize the meat (the acid from the tomatoes).

BEEF STEW

1 ½ -2 pounds beef round chunks—or stew meat, which is chuck
2 cloves garlic, peeled, halved
3-4 carrots, peeled, cut in 1 inch rounds
4 white potatoes, peeled, cut in eighths
2 medium onions, peeled, cut in quarters
1 can peas (15 oz)
1can cut green beans (15 oz)
Olive oil –enough to coat the bottom of the pot—about 1 teaspoon
Salt/pepper/ a bay leaf to taste

In a large—two-handled—pot, heat oil and add beef chunks, garlic and onions.
Brown meat on high to medium high. Brown on all sides, stir to prevent burning.
Salt and pepper vigorously.

Reduce heat to low and spread meat and onions across the bottom of the pot.
Add layer of carrots, then add potatoes on top.
Add bay leaf

Cover –with top fully on—and let simmer for 45 minutes, stirring occasionally—until potatoes are cooked through; meat will be tender.

Add can of peas and can of string beans (with the liquid to your tastes, since the stewing process will create juices as well).
Stir, cover, and remove from heat and let sit for 10 minutes.

Stir and serve. This recipe is good for 3-4 people.

For Brisket or Pot Roast

Brisket or Pot Roast is excellent to cook ahead of time. You can cook it a full day ahead and freeze it. Brisket can be frozen, with excellent results And, if you want to make a special or holiday meal—Pot Roast or Brisket is a perfect centerpiece.

If you're going to refrigerate for a day—or even freeze it—before serving, here's some tips.

- Let roast cool down, move it off stove or to a cool burner and tilt cover to let heat escape. After about half an hour, roast should be cool enough to slice
- Transfer Roast to a plate—much easier than trying to cut in the frying pan
- Hold roast steady with a hand—using a fork will let juices escape
- Slice against the grain—which means meat will not look stringy when cut ("Against the grain" is cutting across the muscle fibers not parallel to them)

Cuts of meat:

For brisket: First cut is good, but if not you can use a lesser cut, and add a little time in cooking.

For Pot Roast: Blade roast or Chuck roast, these are less tender cuts of meat that require longer cooking times, as recipes notes. Always cook "fat side up" to let the juices tenderize meat as it cooks. Blade is fattier than chuck; and Chuck roast is often easier to find. Eye Round—tends to be dry—and I wouldn't use for pot roast.

BRISKET OR POT ROAST

3-4 pounds first cut brisket, with a layer of fat on top
(this will serve 5-6 people, generously)
2 Tablespoons of olive oil
3 medium onions, quartered
2 -3 cloves garlic, peeled. Use whole.
2-3 carrots, peeled and cut in half
2 sprigs rosemary, 2 leaves Sage
Salt and pepper to taste (I use Kosher salt.)

In a two-handled pot with a cover—or large frying pan with a cover—add olive oil to just cover bottom of pan and turn to medium high.

When pan is hot, put in brisket and seat on all sides –this is a noisy process with lots of spattering.

When meat is seared, lower heat to low, add onions, garlic . Cover fully and cook for 15 minutes. Check after 15 minutes to see if liquid has formed, if not add ¼ cup water. Salt and pepper generously.

Add in the carrots at this time. Add rosemary and sage.

Cover fully. With the heat on low, simmer the brisket for 2 hours, checking every half hour or so to see if there is liquid enough to be about halfway up the meat.

At 2 hours, 2 ½, 3 hours, check doneness by poking the brisket with a fork—if the fork slides in with little or no resistance, then the meat is done. The brisket can be taken off the heat and left to cool for 15-20 minutes before serving. Or this dish can be cooled and put in the refrigerator for serving the next day.

To change up the flavors of these "Drummys," try using a pesto marinade.

Pesto –without the pine nuts of course!

5 cloves garlic, peeled, halved
2 Tablespoons olive oil
1 bunch fresh basil—rinsed and left to dry. Basil leaves have to be dry to chop well.
(However, you can't make this pesto with dried basil from a jar.)

Use a food processer—I use a mini one—and put in a handful of basil, some garlic and pulse. It should become a thick paste.
Transfer to a bowl and drizzle in a little oil. Stir.
Repeat until all the basil is used.

Place the chicken drumstick pieces in a roasting pan. Spread the pesto mixture thickly on top. Let it marinate for 30 minutes.
Put chicken in the oven—as is— at 350 to roast for 1-1 ½ hours.
The pesto coating will get crispy and delicious.

<u>High heat method</u>: In a 400 oven, roast chicken for 1 hour approximately

CHICKEN –GARLIC—DRUMMYS

Chicken drumsticks—two-three per person for appetizers
Marinade
For every 8 drumsticks
3 scallions, chopped
Garlic, 3 cloves, peeled and sliced
1 lemon or ½ cup lemon juice
2 Tablespoons olive oil
Salt and pepper to taste

Mix all ingredients in a bowl including chicken
Stir to coat
Let stand for about 45 minutes- 1 hour
Arrange in a baking pan and cover with foil
Bake in 350 oven for 30 minutes, then remove the foil and bake for another 20 minutes
Serve

For a Main course: Use drumsticks, thighs, breasts with bone—"whole chicken cut up" is how it's labeled in supermarket.
All directions same as above.
If more than 8 pieces—bake in 350 oven for 40 minutes, remove foil and bake for another 30 minutes.

Side dishes for Lemon- Baked Chicken can be simple—like a salad and rice. Or roast potatoes—since you're using the oven anyway. Wash and slice white and sweet potatoes and lay on a baking sheet or cookie tin. Drizzle with olive oil and generously salt and pepper. Cook in oven—top shelf—for as long as you cook the chicken.

And, a tip for leftover rice: add a Tablespoon or two of water to the rice and tightly cover with plastic wrap, then microwave. The rice comes out tasting like you just made it.

For a heartier side dish, maybe in the winter, serve the chicken with Escarole and Beans (see recipe) or a side of Minestrone soup.

LEMON-BAKED CHICKEN

Whole chicken cut up—or whatever pieces you like
1 cup lemon juice
2 lemons, halved
Salt/pepper to taste

Preheat oven to 400

Rinse chicken and lay out in baking pan, skin side down
(do not layer)
Pour lemon juice over all pieces
Add ¼ to ½ cup water to pan
Salt/ pepper to taste

Roast in 400 oven for 30 minutes

Turn chicken over to skin side up

Squeeze fresh lemons over chicken and Salt/pepper
tuck lemon half or two into pan
Check that enough liquid in pan, if low, add a little water

Roast for another 30-40 minutes until chicken is golden on top and
when pricked, the juices run clear

A roaster chicken—like the proverbial "oven stuffer roaster" is usually around 7 pounds and plump. And you can always add the leftovers (sliced off the bone) to the recipe for Rice and Beans!

For <u>high heat cooking</u>—a method which is faster to roast a chicken—preheat the oven to 400. Tent foil***over the pan.

Roast for 1 hour with foil.

Take foil off and continue roasting another ½ hour. When pricked with a fork, juices should run clear.

***<u>Note:</u> When making a tent, the foil should not be tight, but allow air to flow around the chicken (or whatever you're cooking). That is, use enough foil to crimp it around the rim of the roasting pan, but still not touch the chicken—to allow that air to flow.

ROAST CHICKEN

Whole roaster (not fryer)—like an "oven stuffer"
1 onion, peeled, cut in half
Preheat oven to 350

Take out "giblets"—liver, neck—packet from cavity of chicken
Cut away excess fat
Let water run through the chicken

Put chicken in a roasting pan, salt and pepper the cavity
Peel and half the onion and put in cavity
Salt and pepper outside of bird
Put about ½ inch water in bottom of pan

Roast chicken at 350 for 2-2 ½ hours (approximately 20 minutes per pound)
When stuck with a knife, juices should run clear—it's done.

Spoons we love.

- Slotted spoon
- Ladle
- Serving spoon
- Serving spoon with a long handle
- Wooden spoon—handle doesn't get hot and makes you feel like a real cook
- Measuring spoons –usually comes in a set, Tablespoon to quarter teaspoon

A secret here: As long as you use the same spoons for measurements you don't have to worry. That is, if you want to use the spoon in your cutlery set: use the bigger one as the "Tablespoon" and the little one as the "teaspoon."
It's all about proportion.

CHICKEN SOUP—TRADITIONAL

1 fryer chicken, approx 3-4 pounds
(giblets—the necks and livers in the little packet— can be rinsed and
thrown in as well)
4-5 carrots, peeled, cut in half or chunks
2 medium onions, peeled, quartered
3 stalks of celery, stripped, washed, cut in half
Small handful of parsley (flat), washed

Rinse chicken so that water runs through –take out giblets packet if is
one—cut off excess fat around openings.
Put chicken in large—two handled—pot (6 quarts)—and turn heat to
high. Chicken will begin to squeak as the skin gets hot, turn a few times
to brown slightly.
Add 1 onion, brown slightly, for a minute . Do not let burn.
Add cold water to cover the chicken, keeping heat on high. Add shake
or two of salt

When water begins to boil—which could take up to ½ hour—turn
down heat slightly and let chicken boil for 10 minutes approx. Skim off
any foam that has accumulated.
Lower heat to simmer. Again, salt, pepper to taste.
Add celery, carrots, rest of onions—Simmer for one hour—
Do not cover pot—if you use cover, tilt it to let vapors escape. Stir
occasionally.
After an hour, add parsley and simmer for ½ hour more—chicken
should be soft, falling apart.

Serve with rice, or small shaped corn/rice pasta

Try substituting Beef Strips for chicken breast. Note that beef cooks more quickly than chicken. So if the chicken stir fry recipe calls for total 20 minutes of cooking the beef will cook in total 15. In fact, Beef Stir Fry is a quick dish to make and serve. The most work is slicing up the onions and the peppers.

In buying the meat, sometimes these strips are called "pepper steak" after an old-time Chinese restaurant dish. Some supermarkets will also call these Beef Fajita Strips.

Note that tough cuts—like chuck or shoulder—won't work for this quickly cooked dish.

You can serve Beef Stir Fry over rice with a salad.

CHICKEN STIR-FRY
(Works with beef strips also)

1 pound chicken breasts –boneless, skinless
2-3 Tablespoons olive oil (or other vegetable oil)
2 medium onions, sliced into medium strips
1 red or yellow pepper, sliced into strips (no seeds)
Salt and pepper to taste

Slice chicken into ½ inch wide strips –Careful with the knife, chicken breasts are slippery

Heat oil in frying pan over medium heat until oil is hot—drop a slice of onion in and hear sizzle.

Add onions and peppers, salt and pepper to taste.
Cover and cook over medium heat for 5-7 minutes, stirring once or twice.
Onion will start to turn translucent, and peppers will be soft.

Add chicken and turn up heat to medium high and cook for 10 minutes—stirring, until chicken is tender to touch and somewhat brown on outside.
- Use a cover on the frying pan, but do not cover fully, tilt it so the steam escapes, to avoid boiled taste.

Turn heat down to medium, and cook for another 10 minutes, stirring gently
Serve over rice

If you want the prettiest plate possible: remove the onions and peppers from the pan before cooking the chicken. Add these back in after 10 minutes when chicken is cooked. This keeps the onions and peppers from getting mushy, but still melds all the flavors.

Tortilla chip coating is easy, fun and delicious. Plus every super-market stocks some kind of tortilla chip.

But if you want to use different coatings, try another easy one: homemade breadcrumbs.

NOTE: Most store bought bread crumbs—in those round contain-ers— have sesame in them. Sesame is a dangerous allergen, so be careful— even if you are allowed to eat wheat.

For homemade breadcrumbs:
Plain Rice Chex. I pulse them in the blender until coarsely ground. (You can also crush by hand.)
Mix in salt, pepper, minced garlic and parsley. And viola! — Flavored breadcrumbs, allergy free.

Roll the chicken pieces in these breadcrumbs to coat them, and then pour the remaining mixture over the top. You will need more liquid in the roasting pan—so put in ½ cup of water for this dish.

Use these for chicken or pork—or to stuff mushrooms: Stuffed mushrooms are an Italian -American **must** on the Thanksgiving table. So you'll need this recipe for breadcrumbs come November.

CHICKEN WITH TORTILLA CHIP COATING
Chicken, drumsticks, thighs and wings

<u>For 10 pieces of chicken</u>
1 12 oz. bag of tortilla chips
1 cup rice drink (I use Rice Dream)

Preheat oven to 350
Rinse chicken and place pieces in a wide bowl
Pour rice drink over chicken pieces, making sure wet on all sides

Place chicken pieces in a baking pan, <u>skin side up</u>

Open chip bag at top
On a flat surface, place chip bag on a dishcloth
With your hands or a rolling pin, ***crush the chips in the bag***
Don't pour out of the bag and crush on a cutting board—too messy!

Pour crushed chips on to chicken, thickly coating them, pat down
Pepper to taste

Add 1/2 cup water to bottom of pan
Bake in a 350 oven for 1-1 ½ hours, checking occasionally to see it there
is enough liquid—if not, add a little water slowly to sides of pan

BBQ sauces we have loved.

Most food allergic people can't find a store-made BBQ sauce that is safe for them to eat. Something—Worcestershire sauce, which has anchovies, soy, wheat, nuts, tomatoes, —or something else shows up on the ingredients list.

Homemade BBQ Sauce it is—these sauces work on pork ribs too. Things to mix—and here's where personal taste is king:

- Honey and vinegar—more honey than vinegar (apple cider or rice are good varieties)
- Molasses—a little goes a long way—smokey and deep flavor
- Brown Sugar—makes a nice rub and caramelizes also
- Maple syrup—sweet and easy
- Chili Powder—nice heat, and you can use it as a rub, not only in a mixture
- Hot sauce—to taste in a marinade
- Ketchup—if allowed—a teaspoon is all you need to make a sauce red-colored.
- Pepper—always!

I mix many of these ingredients together and marinate wings or ribs in it before cooking. Brown sugar I rub on—it's messy but good especially for last minute sweetening.

SUPERBOWL WINGS

For each 10 wings:
2 cloves garlic, peeled, chopped fine
½ cup vinegar –apple cider or white or red
Cup of honey—you'll need more too
Pepper and red pepper flakes if you like

Stir vinegar and honey and garlic together in a big bowl—
Put in wings to marinate—for about an ½ hour or so—turning occasionally to get all wings covered.

Preheat oven to 375.
Place wings in pan—wing part up (so they get browned nicely)
Don't stack on top of each other.
Drizzle more honey over the wings.

Bake for ½ hour, loosely tented with tin foil. Baste once or twice with pan juices and/or honey.

Remove foil and bake another 10 minutes—until browned and yummy.

You can always turn oven up to 400 for last ten minutes.

Chili is one of those foods that you can be creative with. And it's great for a crowd. This recipe is for 4-6 people, so add accordingly.

Add spices you like—hot chilis, cumin.
Other spices that enhance, especially vegetarian, chili: oregano, basil, parsley, cilantro
Add frozen corn –a few handfuls

Chili is great over rice—See recipe for rice—under "R"—and it's also great over a baked potato.

And then there's the **Toppings:**
- Chopped onions or scallions
- Bacon bits
- Red or green peppers
- Avocado (if allowed)
- Sour cream(if allowed)
- Jicama

Serve these in separate little bowls, so people can pick and choose.

CHILI
Basic, Meat

2 pounds ground beef—chuck
1 large onion, chopped
2 cloves garlic, peeled and chopped
1 can (15 or 19 oz.) red kidney beans
1 can (8 oz.) tomato sauce (crushed or peeled tomatoes work also)
2-4 heaping Tablespoons chili powder
Hot pepper flakes/ pepper to taste/ fennel seeds if wish

In a large frying pan, or two-handled pot, over medium high heat:

Put in small handful of beef, chopped onions, garlic
Stir until meat browned, do not burn—(meat will provide fat)
When onions soft, add rest of meat
Brown meat, stirring every few minutes
(may have to pour off some fat—carefully!)
Add hot pepper flakes, pepper to taste—pinch of fennel seeds here if wish
Add half the chili powder and stir

Add tomato sauce—still medium high—stir.
Simmer (bubbling) for 10 minutes and turn off
Add rest of chili powder and stir
Add beans and stir

Let it sit for 10 minutes, uncovered or with tilted cover
Taste—add more seasonings if wish
Serve with rice or with tortilla chips.

Chili is a very personal taste dish: **Add** *spicy heat with a few shakes of hot sauce or more pepper—some people add a few slices of jalapeños.*
Add *sausage to the browning meat for a subtle flavor.*
Note: *Chili keeps well and tastes even better next day*

CHILI
Vegetarian

1 large onion, chopped
2 cloves garlic, peeled and chopped
3 carrots, peeled, sliced into ½ inch rounds
2 green zucchini—scrub skin with hands—cut into ½ inch chunks
1 red, green or yellow pepper chopped or sliced
2-3 stalks celery, chopped (optional)
1 can (15 oz.) of red kidney beans
1 can (15 oz.) black beans
1 can (8 oz.) peeled tomatoes –Italian plum tomatoes are good
2 Tablespoons olive oil

2-4 heaping Tablespoons chili powder
Hot pepper flakes/ pepper to taste/ fennel seeds if wish

Sautee onions and garlic in 1 Tablespoon oil
Add red pepper flakes
Stir
Add in carrots, celery, peppers. Cook for 10 minutes
Add in zucchini and all beans. Stir and cook for 10 minutes
Add in tomatoes and bring to simmer. Simmer for 10 minutes.
Stir.

Serve over rice or with tortilla chips

HAMBURGERS

1 pound ground beef (approx 3-4 burgers)—I use chopped chuck, or you can use 85/15% or 90/10 %
1 teaspoon Olive oil

In a bowl, mix meat and a drizzle of olive oil
Form patties
Salt/pepper to taste

Heat frying pan—medium high
Put in patties, brown on one side—3-5 minutes
Turn and brown on other side, 3-5 minutes
Cover pan fully, lower heat to medium and cook approximately 5- 7 minutes (medium)
Turn off heat and let rest, with cover fully on, for 5-7 minutes
Adjust timing: less time for rare, more time for well done burgers

By The Way—Italian hamburgers can be rolled up into little balls and you have Meatballs!

Meatballs should be fried in a pan over medium heat until browned on all sides—yes, even though they're round. You can then add the meatballs to spaghetti sauce—the marinara 'gravy' (Italianism for sauce) is perfect for meatballs.

After the meatballs have cooked through, add them to the already cooking marinara sauce. Let them cook with the sauce at least 20 minutes, but can simmer away for longer.

You can also add meatballs to an already made sauce—store-bought is fine—but again, let the meatballs simmer in the sauce for 20 minutes to allow them to flavor the sauce and vice versa.

ITALIAN STYLE HAMBURGERS

1 pound ground beef
1 cup puffed rice – or 1 ½ cups Rice Chex, crushed(hand crushing good)
3 cloves garlic, peeled, chopped
Parsley—flat, one handful, rinsed, roughly chopped – or use 2 heaping
Tablespoons of dried parsley
Salt/pepper to taste

Mix all ingredients in a bowl with hands

Form plump patties

Fry over medium heat –pouring off excess fat as necessary—until brown on one side; repeat for other side—about 10 minutes per side.

For Italian burgers, either do not cover, or tilt cover so that steam escapes. You want to have a nice browned almost crust on these burgers.

And, yes, this is the basic meatloaf recipe too!

Rib or Frenched lamb chops are the small ones that are easily picked up by the bone to eat. These are rather expensive, but they look pretty.

Shoulder lamb chops are bigger, and a little fattier, but are less expensive and just as delicious.

Condiments for lamb are:

- The traditional mint jelly—which is very sweet, and very green colored
- Chopped Parsley—which is savory
- Rosemary sprigs—Savory and a good decoration
- Mustard—if allowed, mixed with olive oil and shallots

LAMB CHOPS

Frenched lamb chops – 2-3 per person—these are the little ones which are very expensive

Shoulder chops are a little fattier, but much less expensive and just as delicious— 2 per person is good.

Preheat oven to BROIL
Line chops on broiler pan
Salt them
Broil until sizzling—skin should be getting crispy
Turn over : Salt, cook until sizzling and brown

Take out and let chops rest (they will continue to cook a bit) for 5 minutes
Serve

This is meatloaf Italian style—which means it has garlic and parsley mixed in. And, the bacon wrap locks in moisture and brings the amazing flavor of bacon while giving it a rich crust.

If you prefer a bit more crunch in the filling, substitute Rice Chex for the puffed rice cereal. The chex should be crumbled—by hand is fine—and blended with the garlic, onions and parsley before mixing into the ground meat.

The chex cereal gives the meatloaf more texture than the puffed rice and works better when using ground turkey. Both cereals, however, "stretch" the meat into a bigger meal.

Remember: Store bought breadcrumbs contain sesame!

MEATLOAF

For every pound of ground beef:

2 cloves of garlic, chopped (minced if garlic isn't a favorite)
1 handful fresh parsley, chopped coarsely
1 onion, peeled, diced
1 cup puffed rice cereal—natural brand like Arrowhead Mills
4-5 slices of bacon (optional)

In a large bowl mix together—yes, with your hands
all ingredients above, except bacon.
Salt and pepper to taste

Form a loaf with the mixture
Place in a frying pan***
Wind bacon strips over—side to side—like you are wrapping the loaf
Cook, with cover tilted, on low to medium low for 40-45 minutes ap-
proximately (check inside the meatloaf for doneness—it should not be
mushy)

***Another cooking option is to form the loaf, wind bacon strips around
and place in a baking pan.
Bake in 350 oven for 35-40 minutes

*If you use ground turkey, add a teaspoon of oil to the mixture, since turkey is
not very fatty, and this will help make the meatloaf juicy.*

Minestrone is a traditional Italian vegetable soup, perfect for a winter's evening and great for a crowd. Or just make a pot of it and eat it over a few days, especially since minestrone tastes even better the second day.

For a thicker soup, use a little less –1/2 cup less—liquid, that is the beef broth. For a soupier soup, use ¼ cup more water or broth. Adding in more broth or water, or beans or potatoes is a good way to stretch the soup after the first serving as well.

Pasta –is good in this soup. Le Veneziane is a delicious corn pasta that can hold up in a minestrone. If using pasta, pick a small shape like elbows or shells or fusilli.

MINESTRONE
(Italian vegetable soup)
Great for winter, and better the next day!

2 Tablespoons olive oil
1-2 onions, thinly sliced
2 stalks celery, stripped and chopped
4 carrots, peeled and cut into rounds
4 white potatoes, peeled and cut into eight pieces
2 zucchini—scrub thoroughly, do not peel:
Cut into finger -width rounds
½ a white cabbage, shredded
3 slices bacon (optional)
1 can (15 oz.) kidney beans—add more beans to taste

4 cups of beef broth—which is two packets of bouillon in 4 cups of water. Or just use water.
NOTE: Many canned beef broth contains soy, wheat and milk

Choose a two-handled pot large enough for all the ingredients (approx 6 quarts preferably)

Cooking Directions
Coat bottom of pot with oil and add in onion.
Cook over medium to low heat until the onion is pale and limp—do not brown.
Add the diced carrots. Turn up heat to medium and cook for 3-4 minutes, stirring a few times.
Then repeat this process, adding in one at a time, the celery, zucchini, potatoes.
Once potatoes are added cook 5-7 minutes stirring frequently.

Add the shredded cabbage and again stir thoroughly.
Pepper to taste.

Cook for approximately 10 minutes letting cabbage wilt.
Add broth and stir.
Bring to a Simmer—with the pot cover half on—do not cover fully—for approximately 30-40 minutes. Stir occasionally.
At this time the vegetables should retain their look, but be soft and tender.
The cabbage should be very soft and the broth thick.

Add the bacon slices and stir. At this time, you can cook another 10 minutes or simply stir pot and turn off heat. (Heat from soup will cook bacon sufficiently.)

Add beans and stir—Let sit for at least 20 minutes before serving.

Can add pasta or serve with a safe bread.

NOTES

Pork chops come in rib, loin, boneless and bone in. FYI, boneless chops—or roast—can get dry very quickly.

The cheaper cuts—which are more flavorful overall—are good chops for these recipes. Always buy chops <u>with the bone-in</u>.

The most easily found cuts in the supermarket are: Rib chops, also called center cut rib chop or bone-in rib chop, and blade or shoulder chops.
For a change, use a coating mix for pan fried chops.

Dunk chops in Rice Dream, then dredge in coating mix made of gluten free pancake mix, salt and pepper and dried basil and oregano (approx 1 tablespoon each). Then fry them on medium heat in a frying pan—and instead of olive oil, use margarine to fry these. Tilt cover and cook for 20 minutes. When a crust forms on one side, gently turn over to other side, trying to keep coating intact.

PORK CHOPS

Center cut with bone; two per person
1-2 Tablespoons olive oil— enough to coat bottom of pan
3-4 cloves garlic, peeled and crushed
Salt and pepper to taste

In frying pan, put oil and garlic and heat on medium high—<u>do not let oil burn</u>
Put in chops—hear sizzle, and brown on one side –3-5 minutes
Turn and brown on other side.
Turn heat to low, and cover pan
Cook chops for another 10-15 minutes, turning once

You can add sliced apples for the last five minutes—makes a nice twist on applesauce and pork. Use 3 tart apples—with or without skin—sliced.

Who doesn't like BBQ ribs?

These ribs are good finger food for a party, or dinner just for one. A 3-pound "rack" serves 3-4 people. But make extra! These ribs are so good, people will keep coming back for more. Plus leftovers last 5 days in the refrigerator, and freeze well.

And, then there's "**pulled pork**." Pork shoulder is the cut used to make pulled pork. Again, this is a long, but easy cooking process.

Get a Pork Shoulder, which is about 7 pounds, and is sometime called a "picnic".
Cut up 3 garlic cloves and make little cuts in the roast and stuff the garlic in
Put the pork shoulder—room temperature—in a roasting pan and roast at 425 for 15 minutes, then turn the oven down to 325 and roast for 3-4 hours—or about 25 minutes a pound. The meat should "fall apart to the touch" when ready.

OVEN BAKED RIBS

These ribs are super easy, but they take a while to cook in the oven.

Pork spare ribs — about 4 pounds—which feeds about 4 hungry people
1/2 cup apple cider or wine vinegar
Honey— lots of it!
Pepper
A sprinkle or two of chili powder.

Mix vinegar and at least 1/3 cup honey in a cup. Stir until well mixed.
Lay ribs in roasting pan—and pour mixture over them.
Sprinkle the ribs with pepper and a chili powder—and if you like it hotter—a sprinkle of hot sauce.
Marinate for 30-40 minutes—turning ribs over a few times.

After the ribs marinate, pour off the liquid—but reserve it.
Drizzle a fair amount of honey on them.

Put in 450 oven.
After 15 minutes, turn oven temperature down to 325. Tent the pan with foil, which you take off for last half hour.
Cook for about 1 ½ hours— drizzling honey frequently and liberally.
Baste with the pan liquid also. (If there is not enough liquid, use some of the marinade you kept.)
Take tin foil off for last half hour so ribs get nice and brown.
Enjoy!

Rice is staple that no kitchen should be without. Brown or white, jasmine or Basmati.

NOTE: Wild rice shares proteins with nuts—so wild rice is not a good product for people allergic to nuts and peanuts.

Rice Cookers are a great investment, and even the mid-level rice cookers work very well. In many parts of the country, the super-market–type drug marts sell rice cookers. And supermarkets may sell rice cookers as well.

Rice cookers make perfect rice every time, without you keeping a watchful eye over the pot. Also, a good trick is to steam vegetables along with the rice. This works well for asparagus, carrots, and broccoli to name a few.

RICE

White rice, 2 cups
3 cups water
Dash of salt

Boil water in a pot with cover, dash of salt as begins to boil
Add rice once water is boiling; stir once or twice
Cover and bring to a boil again
Lower heat to simmer and simmer for 10-12 minutes (or until rice has soaked up all the water and is soft in texture)
Stir—take off heat and keep covered for 3-4 minutes

This is a lot of rice—it will serve 4 people generously, and have leftovers.

Rice Variations and Add-Ins

Rice is one of those eminently transformable side dishes or main dishes. Rice can be served alone, plain white or brown. You can put steamed vegetables over it and, viola, a meal.
Or roast vegetables and then put them on top of rice.

You can mix in any manner of items:
- Package frozen mixed vegetables—easy as can be.
- Cup of chopped apples and ½ cup of raisins or dried cranberries—a THANKSGIVING favorite, sweet and delicious
- Frozen peas and/or corn
- Leftover cubed browned chicken
- Tomatoes, canned and cooked down with celery or spices

RICE AND BEANS

1 cup cooked rice—or more. Leftover rice is great too.
1 can (15 oz.) kidney beans, dark red or red
1 small onion, peeled, chopped
½ red or yellow pepper, chopped or sliced
1 Tablespoon oil
Handful Italian (flat) parsley, washed, rough chopped
Cilantro, chopped (optional)

Coat bottom of frying pan with oil and heat.
Sautee onion and pepper, until translucent (approx 7-8 minutes on medium)
Add Rice
Stir, cover fully and cook for approx 5 minutes.
Add beans (with or without juice, your preference)
Stir, add parsley, and re-cover. Add cilantro.
Turn off heat and leave for 8-10 minutes

Add chicken to Rice and Beans and you have a great way to finish off leftovers. If you roast a chicken— see Roast Chicken recipe: Slice meat off the bone, then cut into cubes

Coat a frying pan with a little oil, and on medium high heat, sautee the chicken pieces until browned on all sides, and add it into the Rice and Beans

A friend told me, for salad:
Always use something crunchy and always throw in a little fruit because it gives the salad a fuller "profile."

Use your imagination and your personal preferences.
Salad dressing:
- Always use more olive oil than vinegar (red wine or apple cider or rice wine)
- Add a teaspoon of Balsamic vinegar to sweeten
- Add garlic, crushed, salt and pepper to dressing, not salad
- Mix dressing in a cup or cruet and then dress salad
- Good herbs for dressings: oregano, rosemary, mint, oregano
- Mustard—though only if allowed, it's high on the allergen list—spicy or Dijon makes a dressing a "vinaigrette"

SALAD

All lettuces should be rinsed well.
Always mix in a big bowl.

Options:
Iceberg lettuce, Romaine hearts, arugula, mixed greens
Red cabbage
Endive
Radishes
Cucumbers:
—Persian are the little ones and you can eat the skin (wash)
—European, long and can also eat the skin
—Regular, take skin off and cut into rounds or chunks
Celery chopped
Peppers, sliced
avocado (if allowed)
Hearts of palm
Corn, cut off the cob

Fruits:
Apples, sliced or cubed
Cranberries, dried
Grapes –sliced or quartered
Raisins

PROTEIN TOPPINGS
Chicken breast, sliced or in thin pieces
Steak, sliced
Turkey, sliced
Kidney beans or chick peas (canned)
Lentils – though these are small, so are like a topping

SALAD NICOISE (TUNA OPTIONAL)

<u>Dressing:</u> make ahead of time
½ cup red wine vinegar
¾ cup olive oil
3 cloves garlic—skinned and mashed
1 Tablespoon of Dijon mustard (if allowed)
Salt and pepper
Mix all ingredients for dressing in a cruet—let sit for an hour or so

<u>Salad:</u>
Romaine lettuce— one head—rinsed, dried
2 handfuls string beans, snip ends
3 white potatoes (or 5 mall Yukon golds), microwaved, then peeled,cut
up—between quarters and diced
Red onion—a few very fine slices
1 cup canned, pitted black olives, Rough chopped
Strips of roasted red pepper (optional) (you can use jarred peppers)

2 cans drained tuna
    Optional—if not allowed Tuna
    Strips of chicken—roasted and sliced is better than poached
    Chick peas, canned, drained— a couple of handfuls

Rough chop Romaine (bite size pieces around 2-inches)
Steam string beans until tender but not limp
Microwave potatoes until tender but not mushy—peel and cut
Cool (on counter); as cooling, add some dressing if you wish

Let string beans cool down, then mix in bowl—not your serving bowl—
with Romaine
Add some dressing

Put some of this Romaine/bean mixture in serving bowl
Add tuna and lightly toss

Add some potatoes
Add onion slices
Add some dressing
Layer on more Romaine/ string beans—and repeat

I like to make a red onion design to garnish this salad. It's great for a summer luncheon with fruit and chips or whatever kind of bread/ crackers you can eat.

NOTES

SHEPHERD'S PIE

This casserole is easy and pretty much "no-fault."

1 pound ground beef
½ onion, peeled, chopped
I package frozen peas and carrots (10 oz. box)
4 baking potatoes, peeled and quartered
1/2 cup rice drink (I use Rice Dream)
2-3 Tablespoons margarine—Fleishmann's <u>unsalted</u>. (Optional)

Casserole dish for baking

Brown ground beef and onion in a frying pan until nicely browned
Boil potatoes until soft
Add rice drink and margarine as mash up potatoes in the pot

In the casserole, layer browned meat at bottom. Add a layer of all the peas and carrots— straight from the box
And top it off with the mashed potatoes
Bake at 350 for 25 minutes –it will bubble

You can also make a marinara into a "ragu"—which is the traditional Italian meat sauce.

Sauté garlic in 1 Tablespoon of olive oil and add ground beef or pork. You can also use pork neck bones or pork country ribs – pork lends a sweet rich flavor to a sauce. Sausage also is a nice flavoring.

Brown all the meat. Add in the tomatoes and continue to follow the recipe for marinara.

Here's where you can use a jar of store-bought sauce instead of the canned tomatoes. This is a quick method for making spaghetti sauce, and if you add a little fresh basil as well, no one will ever know.

SPAGHETTI SAUCE

Homemade

Which is not to say that sauce out of a jar is bad—it just needs doctoring, in my opinion. And it is usually too sweet.

A note—if you're of Italian heritage—you call spaghetti sauce "gravy." It's a cultural thing…

Marinara

No meat, simply tomatoes, garlic and basil

3 cloves garlic, peeled and smashed
2 handfuls fresh basil leaves
1 can (28 oz.) Italian peeled tomatoes, smashed with a fork (or your hand)
2 tablespoons olive oil
Red pepper flakes to taste
Salt and pepper

In a large frying pan, sauté oil and garlic over medium high heat.
Add a few shakes of red pepper
Add in tomatoes and their juice—it will spatter
Simmer, stirring occasionally, for 40 minutes.

Add basil, stir, and turn off heat. Ready to serve in 10 minutes.

Knives:

I use a steak knife for cutting everything.

<u>Don't take that advice.</u>

There are entire books just about knives; obviously, I'm not an expert.

Just find a knife you're comfortable with –and be careful. Don't ever rush while slicing.

STEAK

Buy:
Top Round London Broil
(*½ pound per person, remember beef shrinks*)
Sirloin steaks, have a bone in them, also broil well

Preheat oven to BROIL
Place steak on broiler pan

Salt and pepper both sides
Broil until sizzling—top should get brown 3-4 minutes depending on thickness of steak
Turn over : Salt, cook until sizzle and brown
Take out and let steak rest for 5-7 minutes

Slice, in thin strips, against the grain.

VEGETABLES

ACORN SQUASH

1 acorn squash

Cut the squash in half—this is a tough job. Put a dishtowel under the squash so it does not shift while you're cutting it. You may need to 'saw" through it.

Scoop out seeds

Place halves face down (skin side up) on a broiler pan

Roast in 350 oven for 20 minutes

ASPARAGUS

1 bunch of asparagus
1 lemon, cut in half (optional)

Cut —or snap the stems – about 1 inch off the bottom
Rinse the asparagus

In a frying pan, boil ½ inch water, add a few shakes of salt
Place asparagus in pan and cover for 2-3 minutes
Check "doneness"—firm but not hard, not bright green

Remove from pan and put on plate – if the asparagus need a little more cooking, put a cover over the plate for a minute or two and they will continue to cook.

Asparagus can be served room temperature, with a spritz of lemon

BOILED POTATOES, GRANDPA STYLE

4-5 Russet baking potatoes or other white potatoes
Peel and cut into chunks
Olive Oil
Salt and pepper

Boil lots of water in a two-handled pot big enough to comfortably fit all potatoes.
As the water comes to a boil, add salt—three good shakes from the salt shaker

Add potatoes (carefully, with a spoon, so no splashes)
Boil for 10 minutes or until just soft enough for a fork to run through, but not mushy.

Drain the water thoroughly—use a slotted spoon, safety method
Put potatoes in a bowl, lace generously with olive oil, add a pinch of salt and toss gently.
Add pepper generously, and cover bowl with a plate to keep heat in.
Serve soon thereafter.

If leftovers, fry up with sliced onions as a side dish

BROCCOLI – TWO WAYS

Steeped
1 head broccoli
2 cloves garlic, peels, halved
1 Tablespoon olive oil
Pepper

Cut 1 inch off bottom of broccoli stalks, then cut those stalks off the head
Cut, or break, head into florets; cut stalks in half
Strip the hard outer skin off the stalks and the tips of the florets

In a one-handled pot, boil water—enough to cover the broccoli . add a shake or two of slat.
Put broccoli into boiling water and boil for 10 minutes.
Remove with a slotted spoon and put broccoli into a large mixing bowl.
Add in some of the broccoli water
Put the garlic, oil and few shakes of pepper over the broccoli in bowl.
Toss
Cover the bowl with a plate and let this mixture "steep" for 10 minutes.

Eat this broccoli salad as a side dish—which is good room temperature
Or, steeped broccoli is delicious over pasta.

Roasted—with thanks to Emma

Clean one head of broccoli as above
Arrange pieces in a roasting pan, and drizzle oil over them. I use a generous drizzle.
Add a little water to bottom of pan
Roast in a 375 oven for 20-30 minutes—until broccoli is cooked through (check with a fork) and crispy brown on top

CAULIFLOWER A LA SICILIANA

1 head cauliflower
3 tart apples (Granny Smith are good), washed
2 handfuls of golden raisins (Sultanas)
1-2 Tablespoons olive oil
Salt to taste

Preheat oven to 400
Break/cut up cauliflower in "florets"
Slice apples into 1/2 inch slices

Lay cauliflower and apples in a baking dish and drizzle with olive oil
Mix it (yes— with your hands) so the olive oil coats
Sprinkle raisins over the mixture
Add 3 Tablespoons water

Cover with foil
Bake in a 400 oven for 20-25 minutes—remove foil
Bake another 10 minutes, or until the cauliflower is golden brown

ESCAROLE AND BEANS

1 bunch escarole
1 can (15 oz.) Cannellini beans (Italian white beans)
2 cloves garlic, peeled and sliced in half
Olive oil

Cut the hard bottom stem off the escarole and rinse the leaves in a pot of water. Rinse a number of times as escarole can have dirt (yes, from the ground!) on the leaves.

Leave aside to air dry.

In a frying pan, put oil to cover bottom, with garlic on medium high heat. When garlic is golden—not burned—put in the escarole leaves and cover—quickly.

There will be a lot of sizzle and spatter when the damp escarole hits the hot oil. That's good.

After a few minutes turn the heat down to medium, and let the escarole cook for 6-10 minutes until wilted and not bright green. Stir.

Put in the beans—with or without liquid—your taste.

Add a couple of shakes of pepper and bring pot to simmer then turn off.

Stir and serve.

KALE

Kale is leafy green vegetable, best in the Fall after the first frost. And, kale boils down, so as a gauge, use two bunches for four servings.

Plain
I bunch kale

Strip leaves away from stems—that is, in a downward motion, pull leaves off the stalks. Throw away stalks.

Rinse kale leaves thoroughly as it can have grit or dirt.
Fill a pot ¾ full with water and bring to a boil. (Kale likes lots of water to bring out its flavor.)
When water reaches a boil, add kale and push down so water covers all leaves.
Boil 20-30 minutes approx—kale should be dark green—not bright green—and soft.

Italian Style
Follow directions above.

After kale is cooked, use a slotted spoon to remove kale to a bowl.

Add, two cloves, peeled and halved garlic. Drizzle oil generously around the bowl.

Toss. Cover bowl with a plate to let the kale steep with the garlic and oil.

MASHED WHITE POTATOES

4-5 baking potatoes, peeled and cut into small chunks
1 cup, approximately, rice drink –not a flavored variety (or chicken broth)
2-3 Tablespoons margarine (Fleishmann's unsalted)

Boil potatoes, in salted water, until soft.
Drain water thoroughly and with a fork (or hand masher) start breaking up the potatoes

Add rice drink a little at a time, stopping to mix the liquid with the potatoes, which should be getting creamy
Drop in slices of the margarine
Keep stirring in rice drink and mashing until potatoes are the desired consistency—add a dash of salt and serve

For those of you who like super- creamy mashed potatoes, use a hand mixer

QUICK PEAS

1 can (15 oz.) of peas (two people)
1onion sliced
Olive oil –approx 1 Tablespoon

Sauté the onion in the olive oil over medium heat until onion is transparent
Turn heat to high and hear it sizzle
Pour in the cans of peas—with juice
Heat together until the peas just about simmer
Take off heat; stir and add pepper to taste

Serve as a side dish.
Mix into cooked pasta and serve
Serve over rice (with a twist of parsley on top)

REFRIED BEANS
Black or Red

1 can (15 oz.) of red kidney beans or black beans
2 cloves garlic, peeled, chopped
1small onion, peeled and chopped
Olive oil – 1 Tablespoon

Parsley—and/ or cilantro—, handful, washed, stems cut off
Pepper to taste –canned beans have of plenty of salt
Dash of red pepper flakes

Sautee the onion and garlic in a frying pan
Add red pepper flakes

Drain most of liquid from beans
Turn heat to high
Add beans and remaining liquid

Bring to a simmer, and let beans simmer for 3-5 minutes

With a fork mash the beans in the pan, mixing with the onions and garlic
Turn off heat and mash more until a thick mixture
Stir in parsley/cilantro—either whole or roughly chopped

ROASTED ROOT VEGETABLES

- Carrots – peeled, cut in thirds
- Potatoes, white, sweet, Yukon gold . Rinse skin, and quarter or cut into thick slices. For white potatoes, peel them first.
- Fennel – cut the tops off, and halve the bulb or cut into thick rounds
- Onions, peeled and quartered
- Celery, stripped and rinsed and cut in half
- Cauliflower, cut bottom off and break into florets. I like cauliflower with onions and carrots—and see the recipe for Sicilian Style Cauliflower.
- Broccoli—has its own page…

Take pieces of each of these vegetables— whatever combination you like—
And place in a shallow pan. They should not be layered.

Drizzle with olive oil and mix with hands to get vegetables lightly coated
Roast in a 400 oven for 30 -40 minutes –test doneness with a fork— should be soft, not mushy

If mixture includes cauliflower or potatoes,I always cover with foil for first 30 minutes, which helps cook them through, then I take foil off to get the vegetables a golden brown.

THREE BEAN SALAD

1 can (15 oz.)cut green beans
3/4 can chickpeas
3/4 can kidney beans(dark or light)

In a bowl, gently layer or mix the beans

Dressing:
Mix together in a cup
1/4 cup vinegar
3/4 cup olive oil
1/4 Balsamic vinegar (optional)
2 cloves garlic, peeled and smashed
Salt/ pepper
A few pinches Oregano if you like
Stir

Dress the beans lightly— you won't use all the dressing
Leave beans in refrigerator for a couple of hours and turn beans every
so often.

ZUCCHINI — ITALIAN STYLE

2-3 medium green zucchini, rinsed with skin rubbed, cut into rounds
1 large onion, peeled and thick sliced
½ a red or yellow pepper, sliced (optional)
2 Tablespoons
Salt and pepper

In a frying pan, heat oil on medium
Add zucchini, onions, peppers
Salt and pepper to taste
Cook uncovered on medium to low heat, stirring frequently, until the onion is transparent and zucchini is soft.

COOKING TERMS

Bake: To cook food in an oven—called roasting when applied to meat or poultry

Barbeque: Long, slow direct- heat cooking, including liberal basting with a barbecue or other sauces

Baste: To spoon juices over food—to moisten it—during cooking to add flavor and to prevent drying out..

Boil: To cook in bubbling water (212 degrees F)

Braise: To cook first by searing/ browning, then to gently simmer with a small amount of liquid over low heat in a covered pan —until tender.

Bread: To coat with crumbs before cooking.

Broil: To cook under strong, direct heat— usually in an oven on broiler setting.

Brown: To cook over high heat, usually on top of the stove. So called because food gets brown in color.

Chop and Dice: To cut into small cubes of approximately uniform size. Dicing makes even smaller pieces than chopped.

Fry: To cook in hot fat (Yum!).

Pan Fry—or Sautee: To cook in a small amount of fat—oil, margarine—over relatively high heat.

Marinate: To soak in a rub of spices and/or liquids—not necessary to cover —to add flavor before cooking.

Roast: To cook meat or poultry with dry heat in an oven.

Sauté or Pan Fry: To cook in a small amount of fat over relatively high heat.

Scald: To heat liquid almost to a boil until bubbles begin to form around the edge.

Sear: To brown the surface of meat very quickly, in a hot pan—to seal in juices..

Simmer: To cook slowly with liquid over low heat—slow rising bubbles surface—not boiling.—surface should only be broken time to time..

Stew: To simmer slowly, in a covered pot, for a long time, with liquid or juices.

Skim: To remove surface foam or fat from a soup or such.

NOTES

- Most cooked foods will last 3-4 days in refrigerator (if refrigerated after cooking)
- Uncooked meats will last 1 day in refrigerator – then cook or freeze
- Fat –from spilled oil or grease on a burner—can easily start a fire. Be Careful! Always **smother** these flames. <u>Do Not Use Water</u>—makes it spread. Smother with a damp dishtowel—and a pan over it.
- Oil spatters—and can burn skin. Lower the heat if pan starts to sputter and stir with dry utensil holding pan off the heat. Do not add water –from washed vegetables or the like—to hot oil.
- Always make enough for leftovers! That way you don't have to cook as much—if you eat 2 chops, make 4; if you use 1 cup of rice; cook 2 cups.
- Cook meats—roasts or ribs—<u>Fat Side Up</u> Meaning if there's a layer of fat over the meat, that is the top. Do this so as the meat cooks, the fat melts into it keeping it juicy and tender.

AMOUNTS and other NOTES

- 2 chops—like pork or lamb— per person
- ½ pound meat per person
- 2-3 chicken thighs per person
- When having company, always cook for one extra person –always good to have more
- Beef shrinks when cooked—so you need even more hamburger than you think
- Fresh vs Dried Herbs: whatever you can get easily is what to use and you need approximately 3 times the amount of fresh herbs as dried.

Safe Food Allergic Brands

- Fleishmann's UNSALTED Margarine only
- Rice Chex or Corn Chex
- Arrowhead Mills puffed rice
- Wesson "BetterBlend" canola/corn oil
- Olive oil –anything that is pure olive oil—NOT extra virgin
- Rice Dream Original Enriched

ABOUT THE AUTHOR

As the mother of a son with multiple food allergies, Jody Falco has survived the ups and downs of birthday parties and sleepaway camps, substitute ingredients and traveling with food. – And, now, even, College!

She has given presentations on parenting and teens with food allergies, at five of the ten Food Allergy Teen Summits, as well as at other food allergy conferences. Her blog: foodallergyworks.com shares insights about everyday living with food allergies, recipes and more.

Jody Falco is a long-time member and supporter of FARE— Food Allergy Research and Education— and its predecessor, the Food Allergy and Anaphylaxis Network (FAAN).

Please feel free to contact the author by email at:
foodallergyworks@gmail.com

www.ingramcontent.com/pod-product-compliance
Lightning Source LLC
Chambersburg PA
CBHW081544040426
42448CB00015B/3215